SAVE THE EARTH
MAZE BOOK

Roger Moreau

SCHOLASTIC INC.
New York Toronto London Auckland Sydney
Mexico City New Delhi Hong Kong

ISBN 0-439-06494-5

12 11 10 9 8 7 6 5 4 3 2   9/9 0 1 2 3 4/0

Printed in the U.S.A.   40

First Scholastic printing, January 1999

Contents

Introduction

The great planet Earth we live on has in the past been called many names that have described its condition. They were friendly, healthy names like the "Good Earth" and "Mother Earth." We could take comfort in knowing that Earth could sustain us and provide for us. In recent times, however, our planet has taken on a new name, a name which is both depressing and frightening. It describes an Earth that is in grave danger, an Earth that may no longer be able to provide for or sustain us. The Earth of today is called the "Endangered Earth."

The Earth is in danger because of the negligence and carelessness of man. Such problems as air pollution, acid rain, water pollution, toxic waste, species extinction, fisheries depletion, deforestation, and radiation peril are just a few of the man-made problems. If something isn't done soon to end the mistreatment, it will be too late to save planet Earth.

On the following pages, you will learn about some of these problems; but of more importance, you will have a chance to do something about it. If you are successful, you could help in taking a great step toward saving Earth!

For practice start with the cover, where smoke from a careless fire is covering the sky. Carry the water through the jungle and up the mountain to put out the fire.

It will not be easy. Nothing worth having comes easily. So don't give up. Face each problem with courage and determination and when you succeed Mother Earth will thank you.

Suggested use of this book: Rather than use a marker on the mazes in this book, use a pointer so you will not give away your work. Then you can reuse the book at a future date or see if one of your friends can be as successful as you are.

Oceans and Streams

Water pollution from acid rain, fertilizers, and urban runoff has affected our oceans and streams. Combined with overfishing and our altering of the natural flow of rivers, these man-made problems endanger wildlife and threaten the ecological balance. The mazes on the next few pages present some of these problems.

SAVE THE DOLPHIN

A dolphin is entangled in some rotting gill nets. You can save it by finding a clear pathway through the rotting nets and untangling it.

FREE THE FISHES

In this overfished area several fish are hooked and snagged on the bottom. They will die if you don't find a clear path down to them between the lines and hooks.

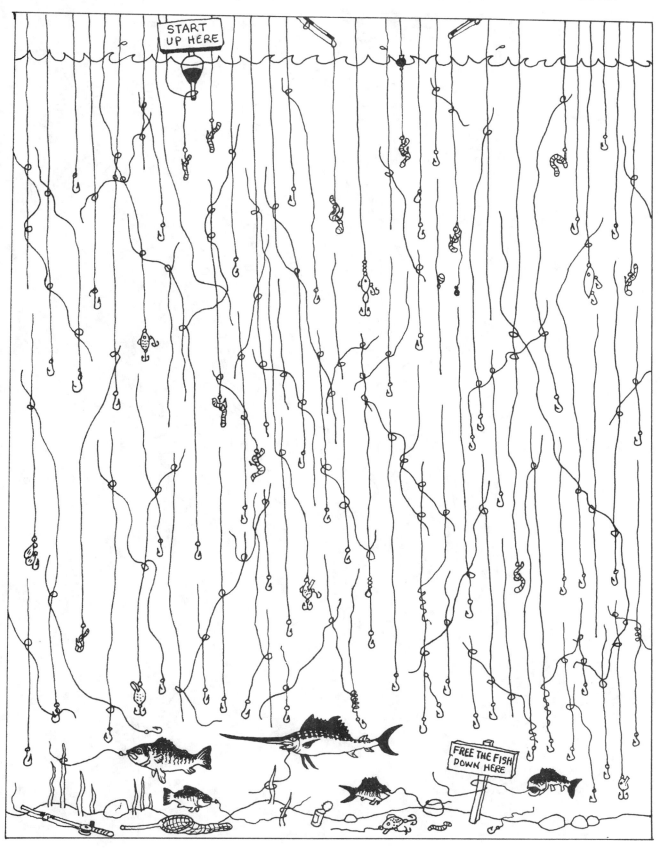

HELP THE SALMON

The river has been dammed many times. The dams confuse the salmon that want to

START HERE

return to where they were born to lay their eggs. Help them find a way around the dams to reach the stream.

FREE THE WHALE

This whale lost its way while migrating south. It turned into San Francisco Bay and

swam up the creeks that flow through the marshes at the back of the bay. Help him find his way back to the ocean.

PREVENT ATOMIC TESTING

This island in the South Pacific is to be sacrificed in an atomic test that will kill all

START HERE

wildlife, destroy the island, and pollute the ocean. Hurry up and find your way to the bomb and pull the fuse.

HELP THE TURTLE

Some turtles are almost extinct. This sea turtle, hatched from an egg on land, must get to the ocean to survive. Help him past the many predators that lie in wait for him.

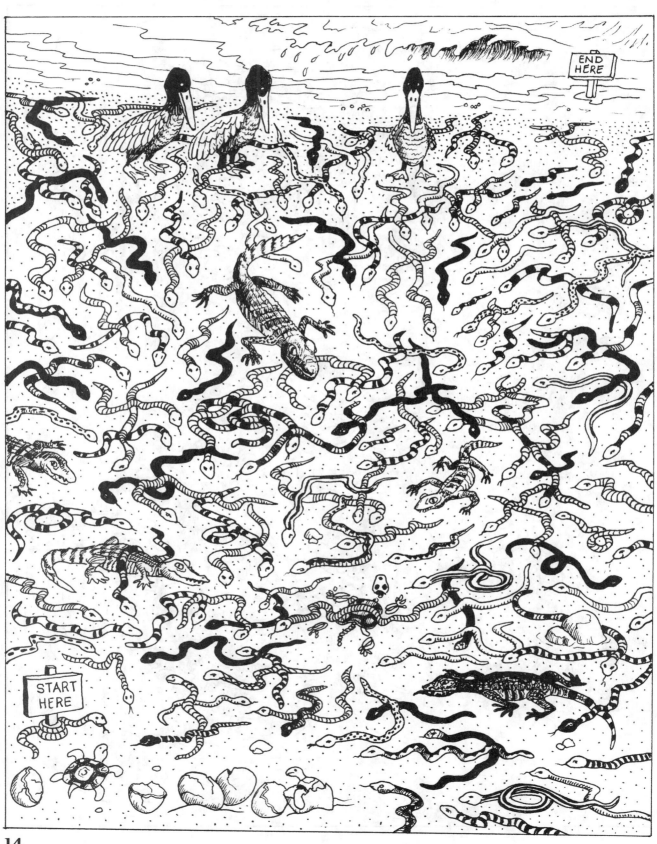

Wildlife

Many species of wildlife throughout the world are endangered because of the carelessness of man and because of shrinking environments. Man must intervene and become actively involved to save some species. The following mazes present some of the problems and give you a chance to help.

HELP THE DUCK FAMILY

This mallard drake and hen want to return their young to the nest. Help them find a clear channel to the nest.

START HERE

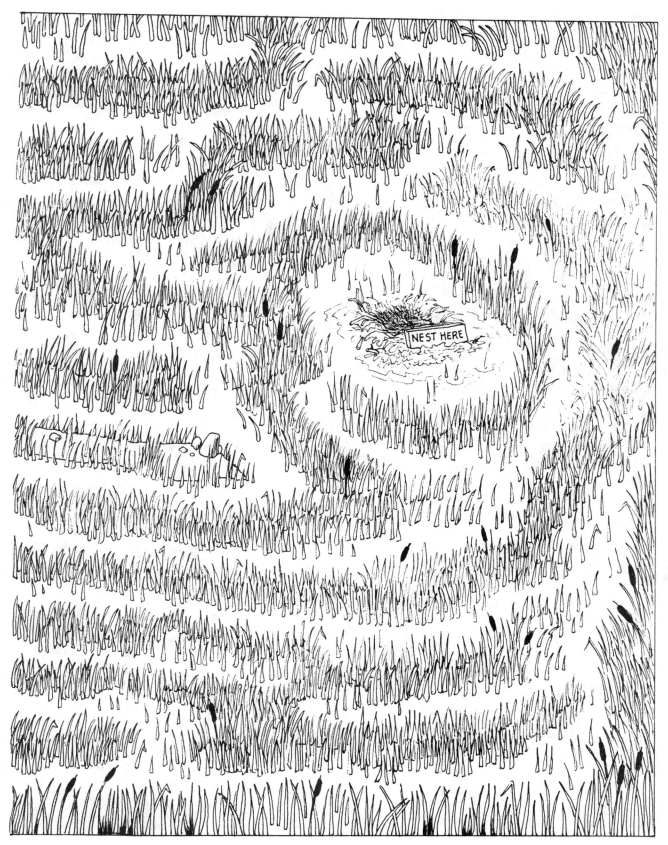

WATERPONDS FOR WATERFOWL

Migrating waterfowl need waterponds to feed and rest in. Waterponds across the country have been disappearing every year. This farmer will let you dig a waterpond

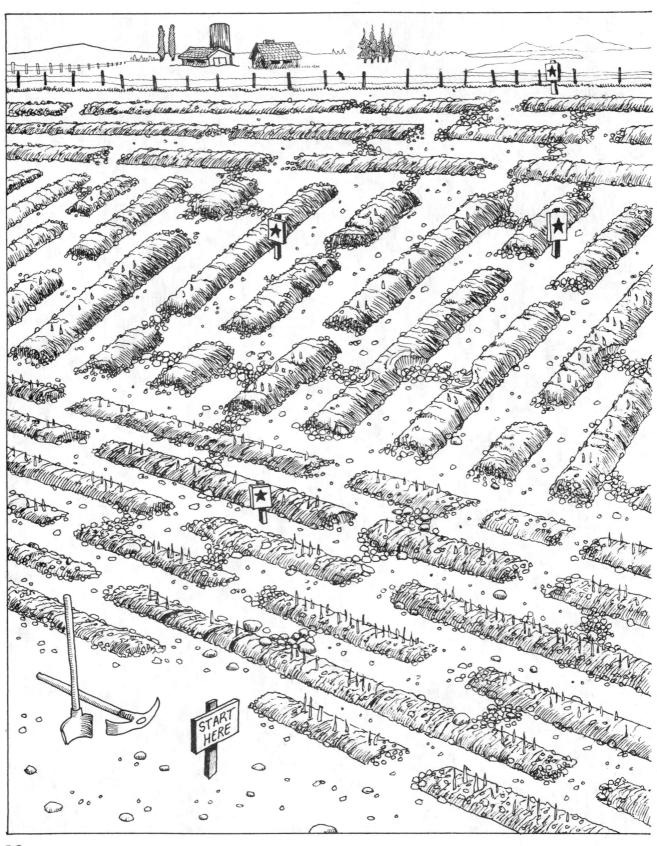

at each place he has put a star sign. Find a clear path and dig a pond at each sign. Do not backtrack. When you get to the water valve, flood the field to fill the ponds.

SAVE THE SPOTTED OWL

Save this family of spotted owls by finding a clear path to them and take them to an uncut forest.

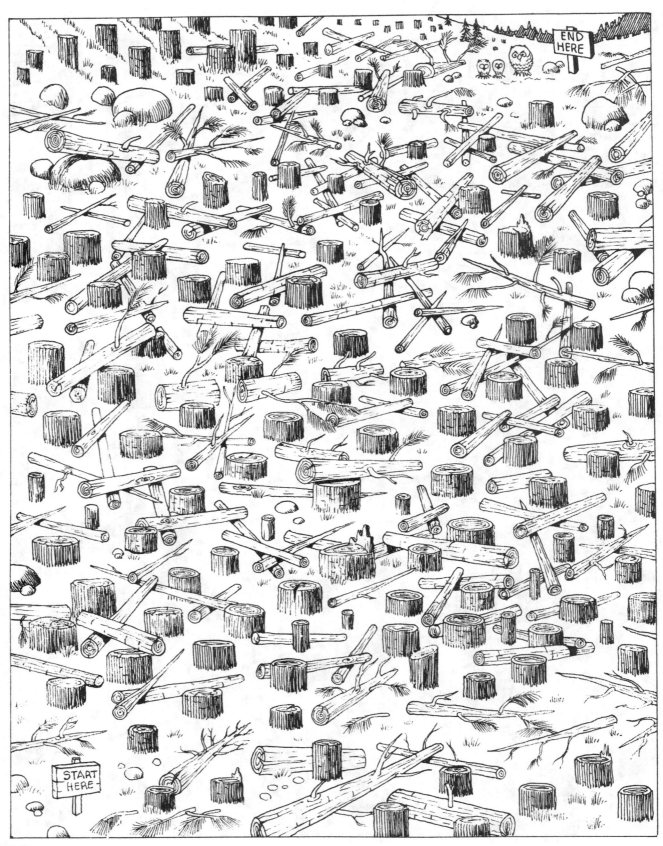

FEED THE BABY EAGLES

Every eagle is a treasure. These babies have lost their mother. Find a clear path up the trail, climb the tree, and feed them.

SAVE THE ELEPHANTS AND RHINOS

Animals with ivory tusks are endangered and are protected from hunting. But poachers, men who hunt against the law, try to kill them to sell the ivory. Another

way to protect these animals is to cut off their ivory tusks. This does not hurt the animal, and they will not be hunted. Save the elephant and rhinos by finding a clear path to them and cut off their tusks.

ARREST THE POACHER

This mountain gorilla is in grave danger. A poacher waits in hiding. Find a clear path and arrest the poacher.

SAVE THE RAIN FOREST

This rain forest is in danger of being cut down. Cutting down the rain forests

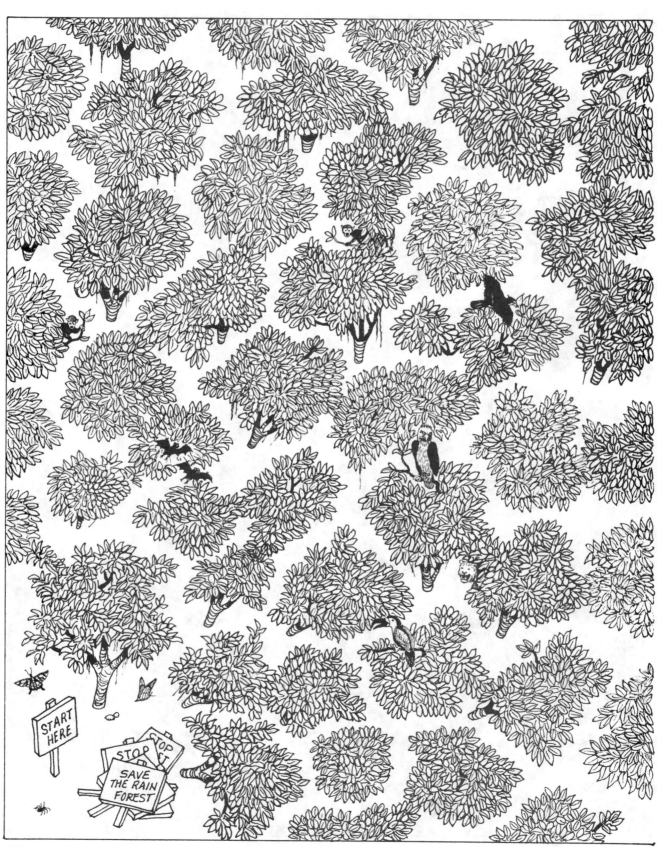

threatens life on the entire planet. Find a clear path and put these signs where the cutting crew has left their saws.

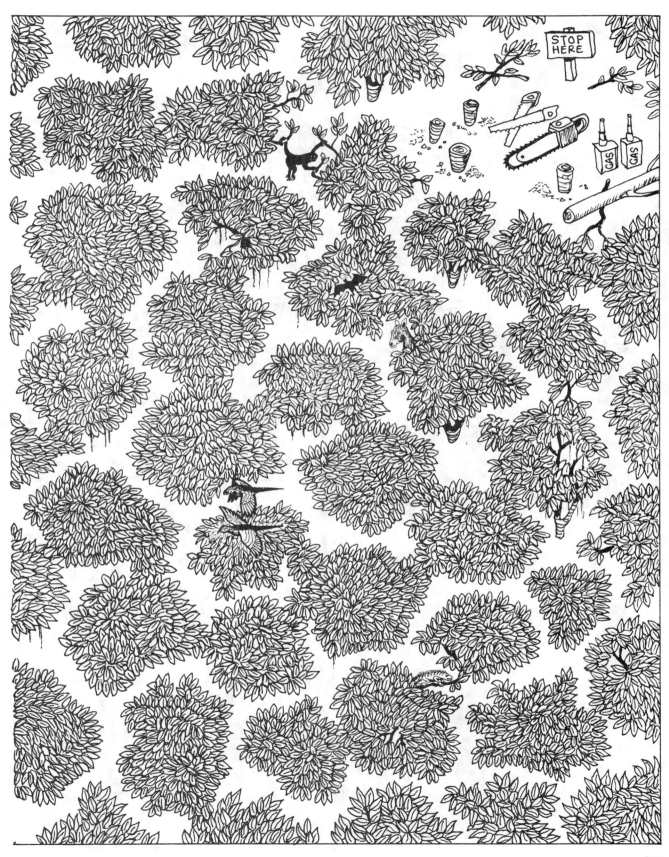

SAVE THE PANDA

Pandas are almost extinct because they are slow to get together and produce

offspring. They sometimes die off faster than they reproduce. Help this male panda find a clear path to the female in the upper right.

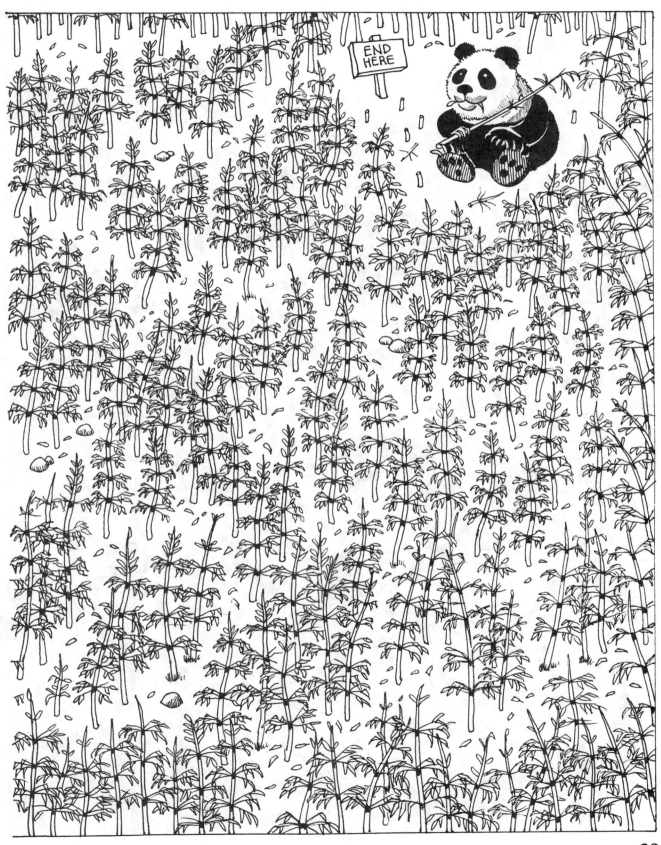

SAVE THE CALIFORNIA CONDOR

Only a few California condors exist, raised in captivity. Some have been released into the wild. Help them survive. Find a clear path to the cave and leave the condor food.

Pollution

Man's carelessness has polluted the earth so much that man himself is in danger. We dump and spill pollutants into the water and onto the land. Acid rain is caused by pollutants that get into the air and fall back to earth in the rain. These pollutants kill fish and wildlife. We must stop pollution and clean things up if we are to survive.

FIGHT THE OIL SPILL

This oil spill is a big mess. To save the birds and seal that are covered with oil, you must quickly find a clear path through the mess.

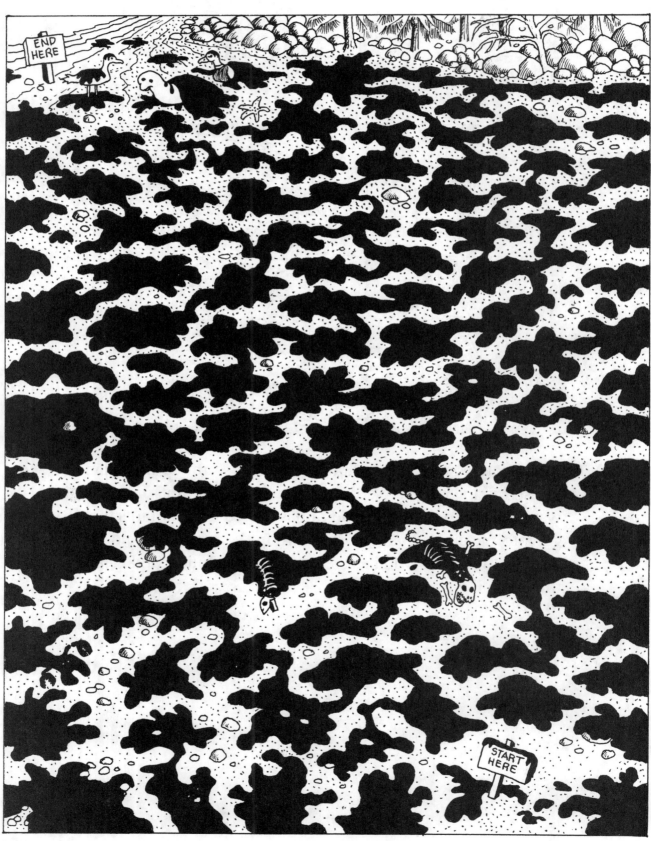

The white bricks stick out just enough from this pollutant spewing chimney so you can climb to the top and put a filter on it. Climb only on the connecting white bricks.

STOP NUCLEAR WASTE DUMPING

These trucks are going to dump radioactive waste into the canyon. Get up the trail in a hurry and stop them. Time is short. Hopefully, you'll be right the first time.

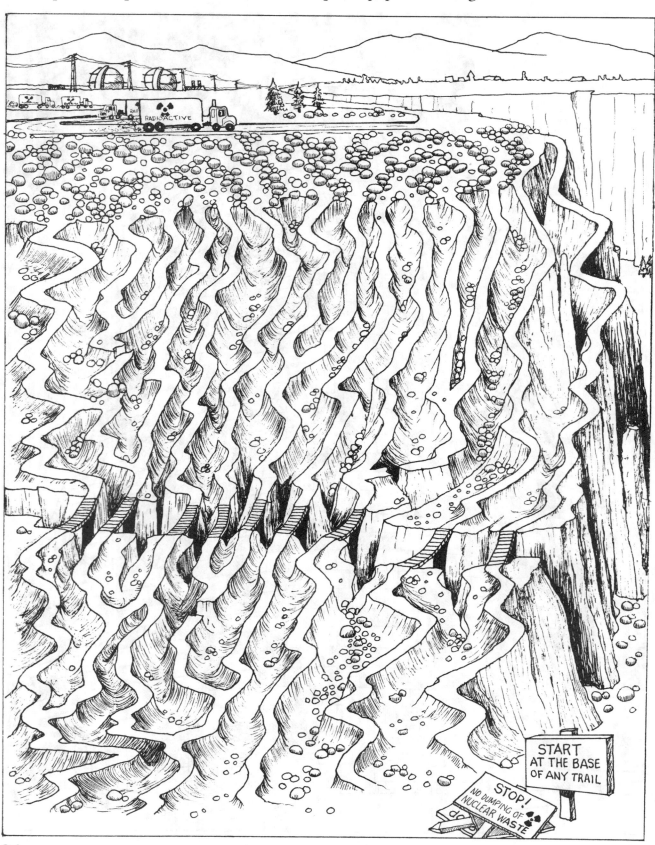

CLEAN UP THE PARK

The junk littering this once beautiful picnic area needs to be hauled away, but the removal truck is broken down. Find a clear path through the field and fix the truck.

STOP LAKE POLLUTION

This pipe is leaking toxic, industrial waste. Put the cork in it to stop the pollution of

this freshwater lake. As you row, find your way through clean white water. Do not get any pollution on you or the boat.

PRODUCE FRESH DRINKING WATER

Place clean ice blocks from the high mountains into the funnel and find your way
down the pipes to open the valve and fill the bottles. It is OK to go behind other pipes.

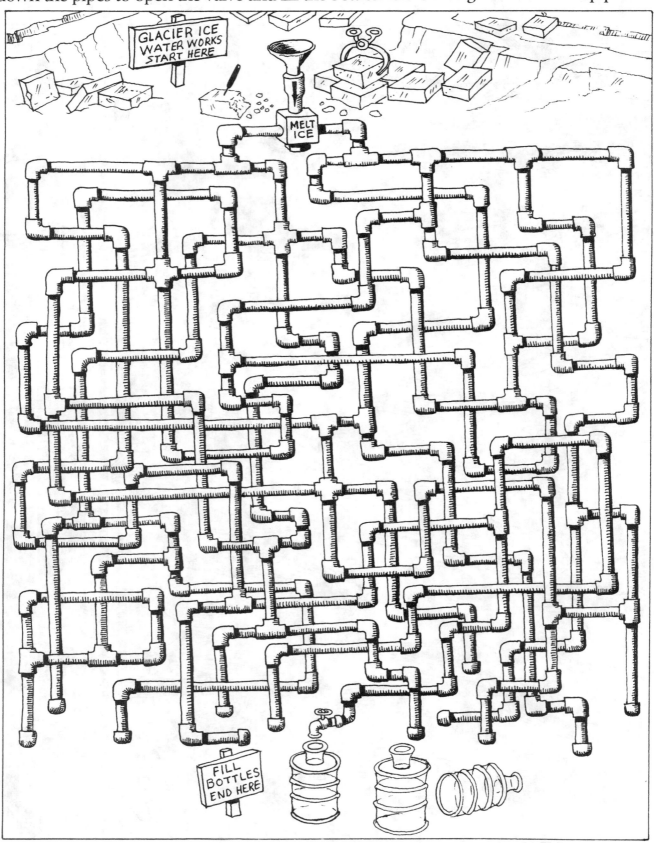

STOP AIR POLLUTION

A van on this freeway is polluting the air. Take the patrol car and arrest the driver. Be careful you don't get off on the wrong freeway.

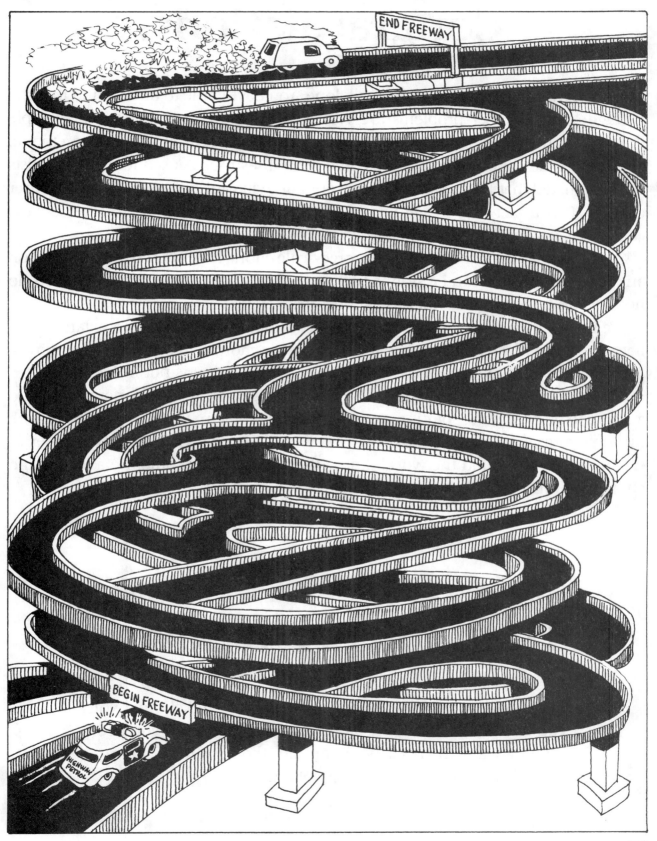

Congratulations!

Mother Earth thanks you for a job well done. You have come to understand that she is fragile and that her problems are very serious. More than two billion people throughout the world lack safe drinking water. Increased carbon dioxide, methane, and other gases in our atmosphere could have disastrous consequences. Scientists have estimated that 1.2 million species of animals will vanish during the next quarter century. It is a fact that it will take a worldwide collective effort to reverse such conditions if we are to save the Earth.

Some people have already started. Large-scale efforts have shown that soil erosion and land destruction can be stopped when a real effort is made. Tropical forests do not have to be leveled in order to feed people.

We have all the resources we need to start bringing our world into balance with nature. Many countries have been increasing their efforts to recycle waste, eliminate air pollution, and manage natural resources. The situation is not hopeless.

To save the Earth, it takes people who have courage, strength, self-motivation, and a desire to be part of the solution—not part of the problem. You have demonstrated, through your efforts in this book, that you have these characteristics and concerns. As you work to rebuild the world, know that the time has come. Be a leader and encourage others to follow your example.

Good luck.

Help for Earth Savers

The world's problems are difficult. It is not unlikely that you could have run into some problems along the way. If you need help or want to check how you did, the keys to the mazes, including the one on the cover, follow.

Save the Earth

41

Save the Dolphin

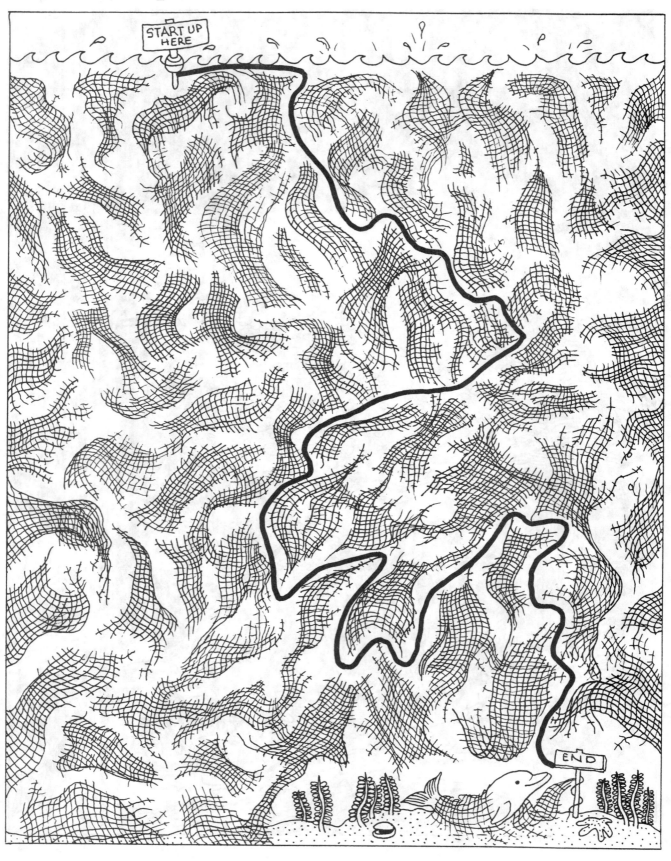

Free the Fishes

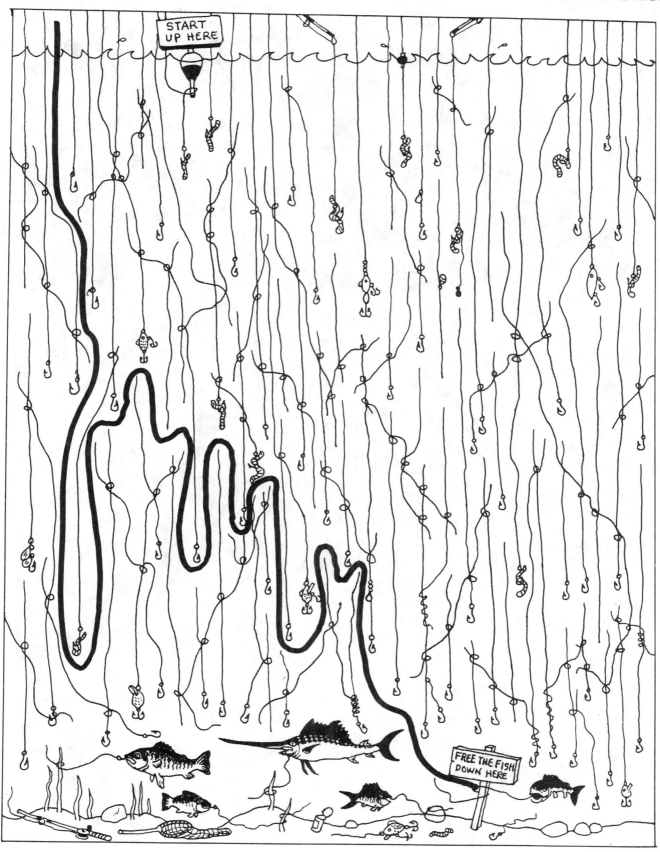

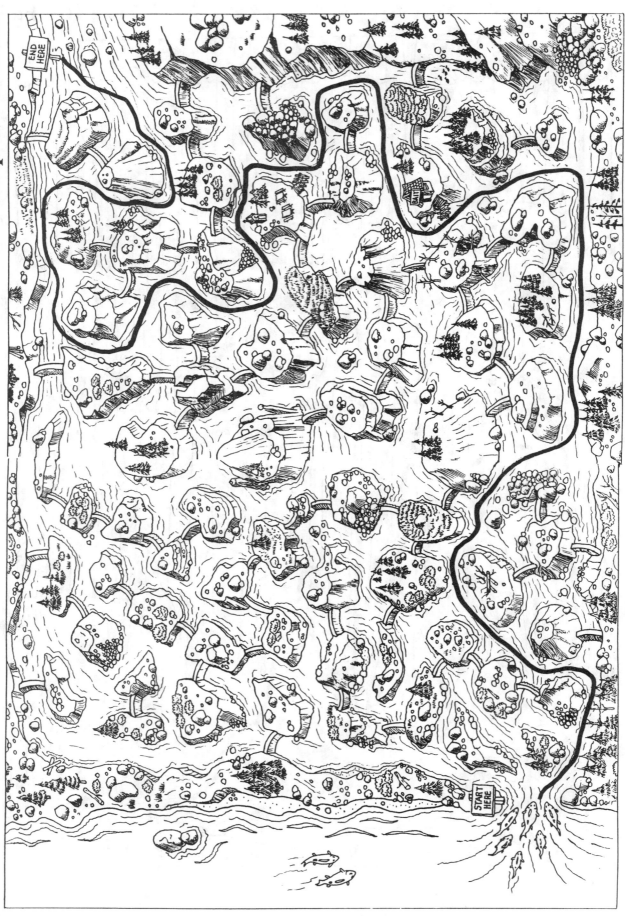

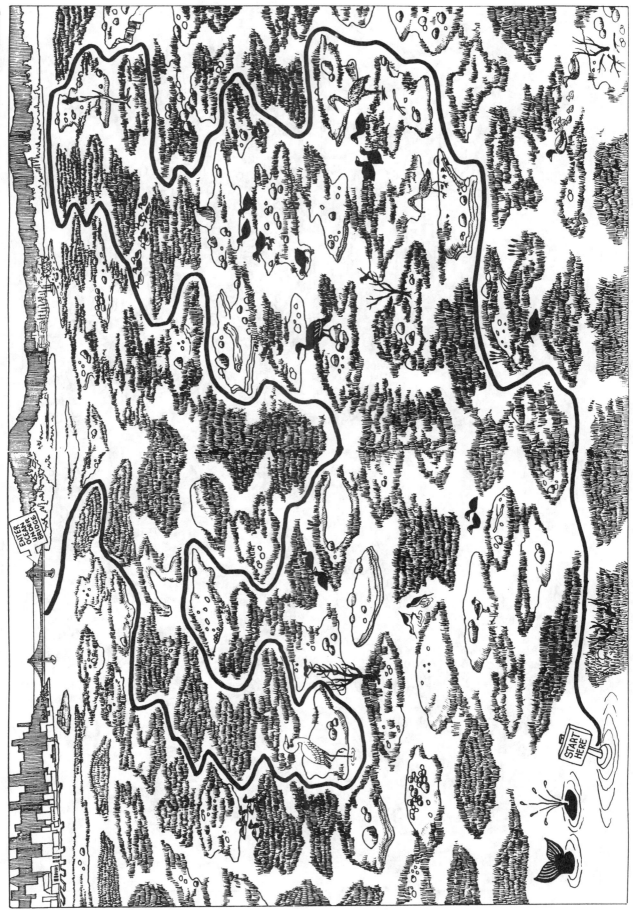

Help the Turtle

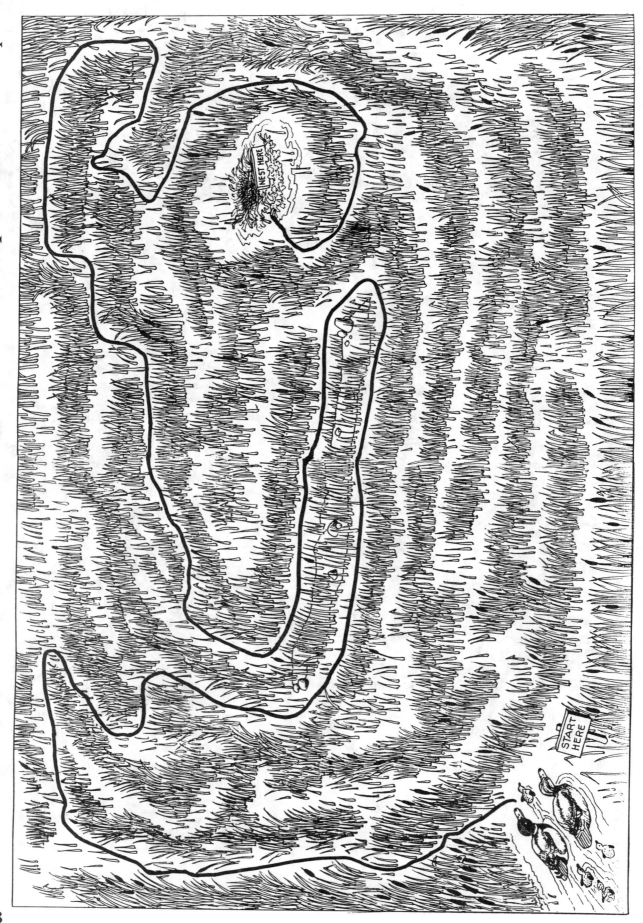

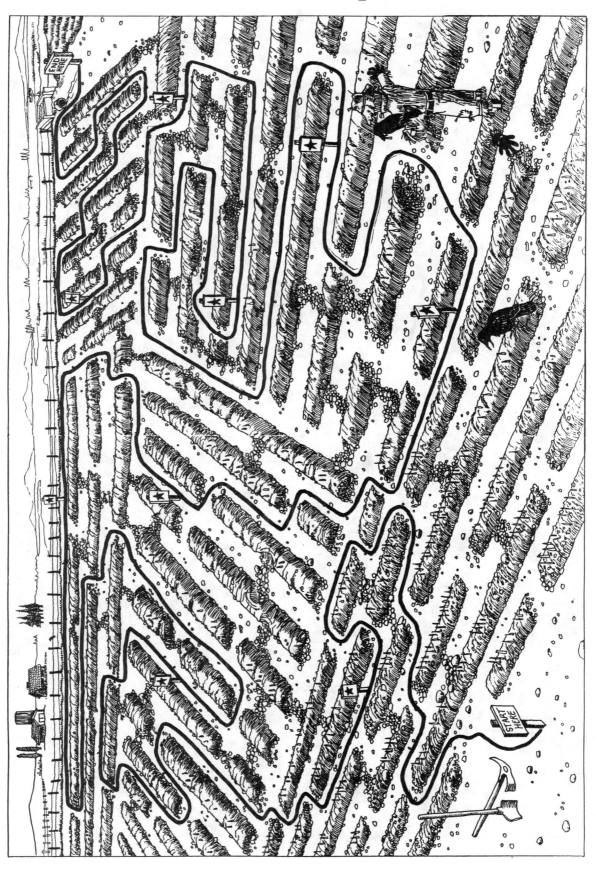

Save the Spotted Owl

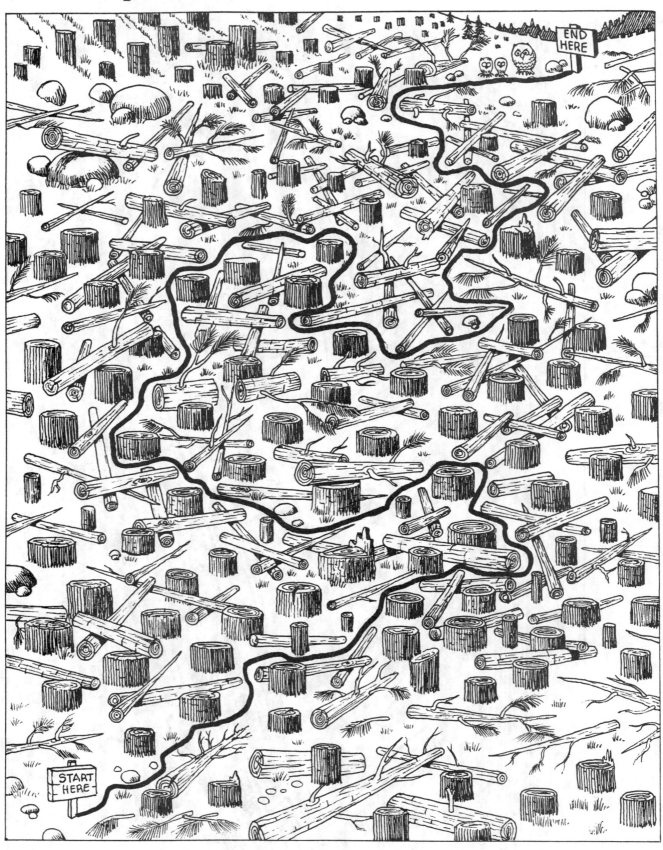

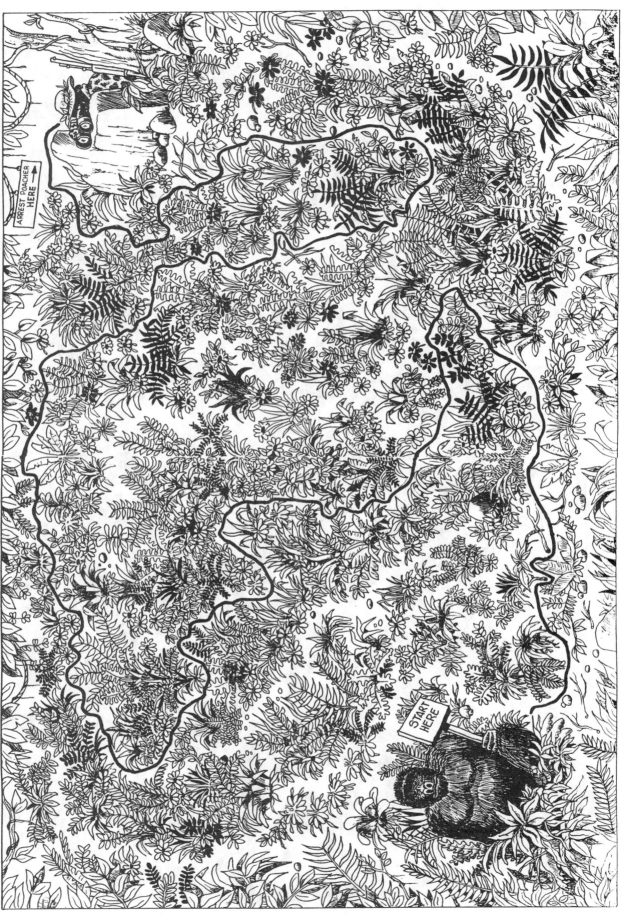

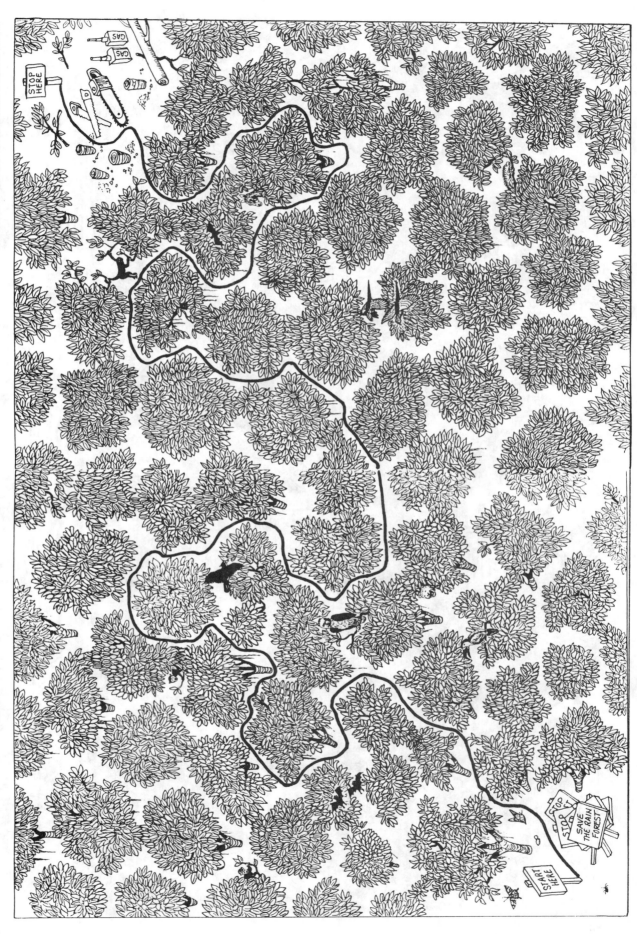

Save the California Condor

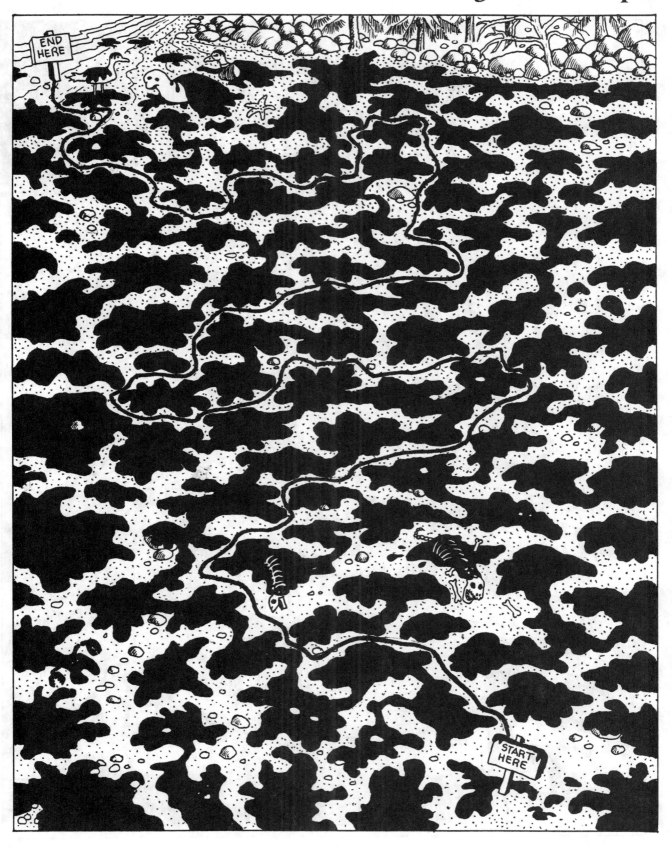

Stop Acid Rain

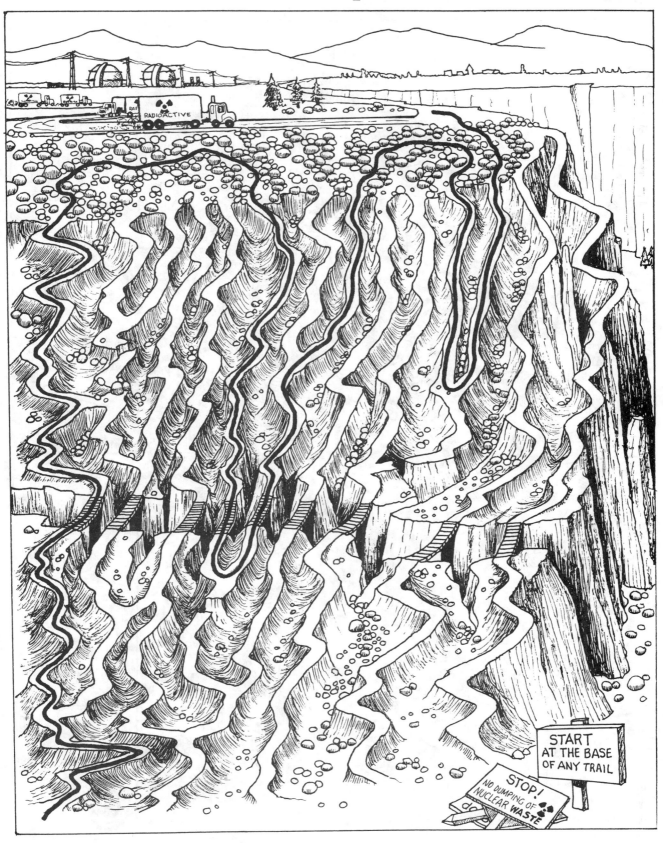

Clean Up the Park

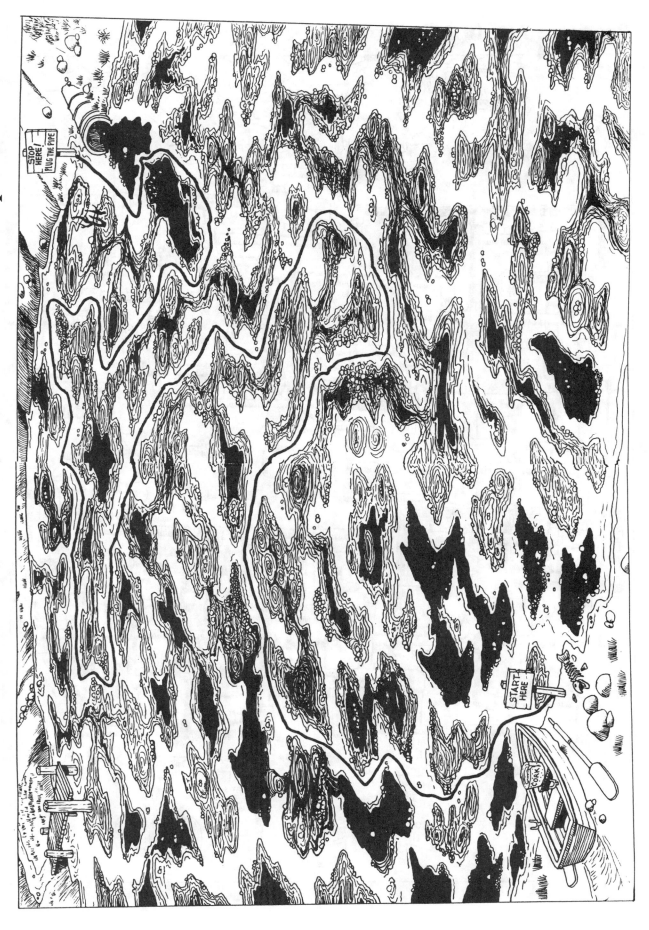

Produce Fresh Drinking Water

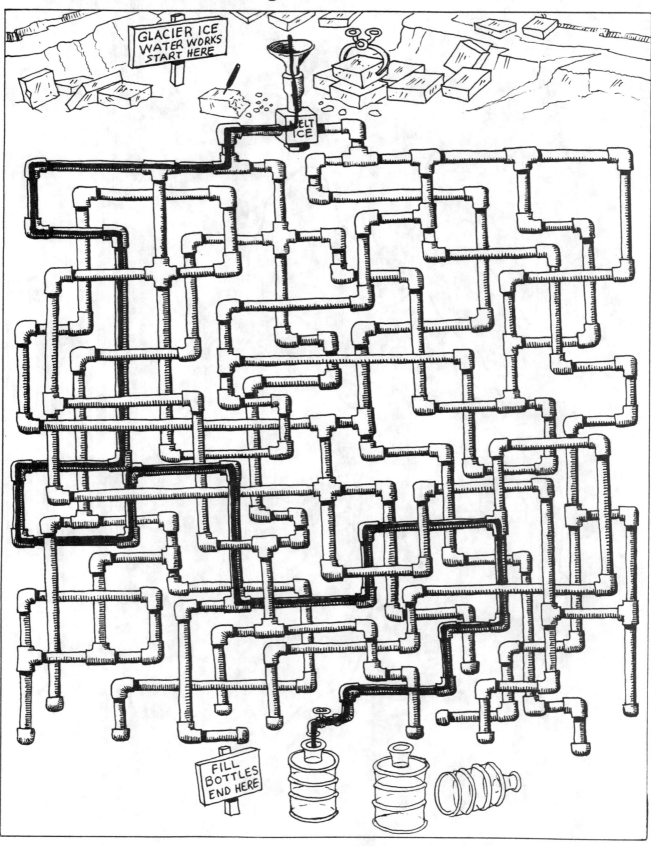

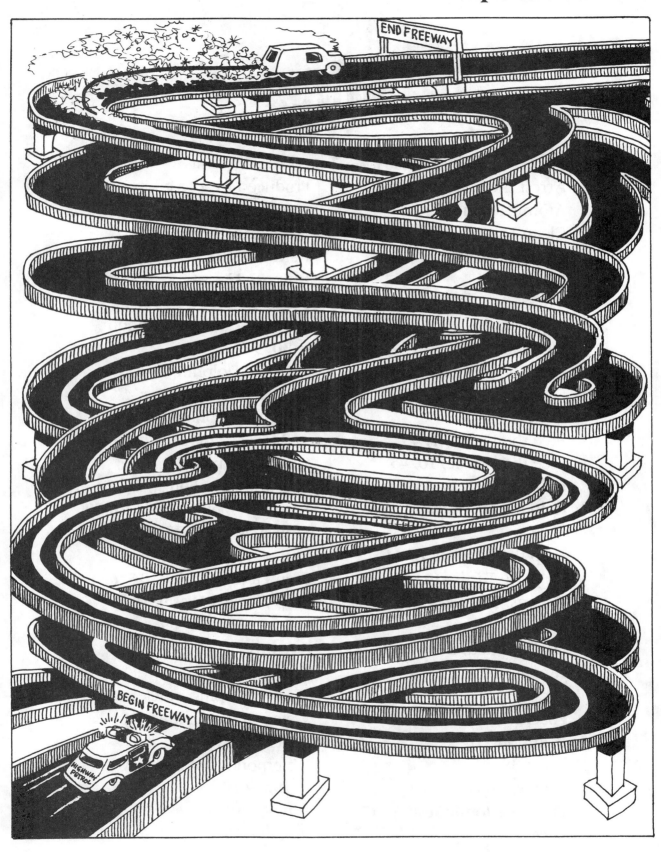

Index

Numbers in **bold** refer to puzzles, in *italics* to solutions.